THE TRANSFORMATIVE POWER OF "THE WORD"

Laurie Benoit

Redemption's Story Publishing, LLC
Houston, Texas (USA)

The Transformative Power of "The Word"

Copyright © 2019
Laurie Benoit

All Rights Reserved.
No portion of this publication may be reproduced, stored in any electronic system, or transmitted in any form or by any means (electronic, mechanical, photocopy, recording, or otherwise) without written permission from the publisher. Brief quotations may be used in literary reviews.

ISBN 13: 9781070404622
Independently Published via Kindle Direct Publishing

For information and bulk ordering, contact:
Redemption's Story Publishing, LLC
Angela Edwards, CEO
P.O. Box 62287
Houston, TX 77205
RedeemedByHim@Redemptions-Story.com

Dedication

*This book is dedicated to each and every person, for we are **all** survivors.*

We are not on the same journey, but we can all strive to become the best version of ourselves.

The Transformative Power of "THE WORD"

A Special Dedication to and In Memory of

Charles Harris (aka "Chuck")

To the father I never had, but always wished I did.

A man whose love was larger than life,

And with him stood, was Momma, his devoted wife,

Whom they believed in the ways of old,

Simple respect and with them both, a heart of gold.

But as your final day has passed,

The flags in our hearts fly now at half-mast.

You may be gone but will never be forgotten.

Acknowledgements

There are so many people in my life today whom I am grateful to and for. If I miss anyone in the following mentions, I do hope you can forgive me.

First of all, I wish to express my deepest love and gratitude to my **Husband** for accepting me with all my imperfections and for holding onto me when life was unbearable. Thank you for helping me to grow through some of our best and worst times. I love you with all of my heart.

To my **Children** who have watched me grow as a person through their lifetimes, I am thankful for your patience and understanding as I learned each day how to be a parent and (hopefully) a better person for you to look up to. I can't tell you enough just how very much I love you *ALL*.

To my very long-time friend, **Todd**: Thank you for helping me to grow through some of the worst times in my life and for giving me that second chance I might not have had without you. For always believing in me, especially when I didn't, **Thank You.** I love you.

To my very oldest and dearest friend, **Cathy**: You could never possibly know how much I have always admired you and appreciated your kindness throughout some of the toughest years in my life. I love you.

To **Dear Lois**: I never really ever told you how much you meant to me while you worked with me and how much those magical words you said to me so many years ago inspired me and invoked strength in me. Thank you!

To **Dear Edgar**: You are truly a humanitarian and as humble as they come. You will never admit your doings, but they don't go unnoticed. Had I not crossed ways with you, I'm not certain I would have evolved enough to find my path here all on my own. Thank you so very much. I wish you all the love you extend to others tenfold.

To my unnamed friends and supporters from the community in which I live who have supported me through this journey: I love and appreciate you so very much. From the bottom of my heart, I thank you **ALL**.

To my Publisher, Editor, and Friend, **Angela Edwards**: It has truly been my pleasure working with you on not just this, but several literary projects. You are such an inspiring woman. Without your belief in myself and others, many would not see the hope you invoke in all you cross paths with. I truly hope that karma really does happen because you deserve much greatness for your humanitarianism. May life continue to bless your inspiring journey.

Lastly, to the few people who are unbeknownst to me and who ultimately decided that my words were enough of value to share across social media platforms and other avenues: I am forever grateful. Thank you.

Introduction

The Law of Attraction is real. This, however, is **not** another Law of Attraction book. This is my true-to-life testimony with the message that you can attract to your life all that love and goodness you both want and desire. Although bad things do happen to good or great people, they can be overcome.

It is my testimony that dreams really can come true!

But (yes, there is a 'but') it doesn't come for free. Breakthroughs require a few crucial elements:

- ✓ Desire.
- ✓ The tiniest glimmer of hope.
- ✓ Belief.
- ✓ Belief in yourself, others, and the universe.
- ✓ Facing your fears.
- ✓ Perseverance.
- ✓ Most of all, it requires that you start —
    - o Start to work on yourself.
    - o Accept yourself — **ALL** of yourself, flaws and all.

When you do all of those things as you work towards the life you want, your dreams and hopes are, in fact, attainable!

One of my favorite quotes is by Sri Nisargadatta Maharaj:

"You will receive everything you need when you stop asking for what you don't need."

How true! When you focus on your goals instead of what you lack, that which you **NEED** will materialize…and sometimes, rather quickly. I am living proof of that! Within four short years of truly beginning my journey, here I am writing to you.

My dream became a reality!

It has taken a lot of work, tears, thought, and willingness to face my fears and overcome them. If I can do it, I surely know you can, too!

Life is filled with experiences, yet it has taken me most of my life to understand that *IT IS WHAT WE DO* with them that matters most.

LIFE ISN'T FAIR. Again, I am living proof of that, too.

Still, no matter what life has dealt you, only **YOU** have the power to choose whether to stay 'stuck' and wallow in your life **OR** follow your dreams, face your fears, and overcome those experiences.

Not everyone has lived a life like mine. Some are better; others are worse. Nonetheless, we all face our own challenges, experiences, and trials in life.

The question is:

*What will **YOU** choose to do?*

The following is just a small bit of what I chose:

THE WORD

A powerful tool that can bring us to feel a million emotions,
Can spark imagination and inspire action
That requires deep thought before we do;
Can create relations or end them,
Yet deserves the utmost care,
For its power is often underestimated
And is what we are passing on to our youth.

So, be gentle…for we **never** know who is listening.

Table of Contents

Dedication vi

A Special Dedication to and In Memory of vii

Acknowledgements.. viii

Introduction xi

Chapter 1

Just Another Writer..1

Chapter 2

A Long, Long Time Ago..11

Chapter 3

Another Sense of Time (The Early School Years) 17

Chapter 4

Woman or Child? 27

Chapter 5

Hope for a New Life 35

Chapter 6

A New Beginning? 43

Chapter 7

To Be or Not to Be..51

Chapter 8

Just a Small-Town Girl..57

Chapter 9

Once in a Lifetime 65

Chapter 10

Life Isn't Fair 73

About the Author 80

Appendix 81

Chapter 1

Just Another Writer

Oh, the **heaviness**! Are you familiar with that sense of heaviness that never goes away? What do I do with this heaviness? I'm so tired of carrying it...

Upon meditating came my answer.

Honestly, I knew my answer all along. It had been with me even in childhood. I knew what I needed to do, but deep down, all of the negativity thrown at me throughout my life kept me from even trying. If it wasn't me wallowing in the negativity, it was every terrible, awful remark ever made to me that would replay over and over again in my mind:

"Your life is insignificant."
"You will never amount to anything [especially without a high school education]."

I dabbled a bit here and there throughout my life. I was even told by a handful of people that I was truly an artist with words. Deep down inside, however...I could never find the truth in their words. Why? Because it was mostly when I was really hurt that my thoughts and feelings poured from my soul onto the paper that sat before me. That was the place I felt safest to openly express myself…most of the time.

I can say with a certain level of surety that we all have written something that has been used against us. It could be something as simple as a note to a special someone in school that somehow fell into the wrong hands, the Valentine's Day card with a special note that was shared publicly for whatever the reason, or even a private letter that someone didn't have the permission to read but read it anyhow.

Maybe it was a poem that you dreaded sharing in class that you were forced to read aloud.

Maybe—*just maybe*—it was all of the above.

The point here is that we all have a humiliating story or two, yet we manage to live life regardless.

BUT when you start writing…

- ❖ Because you want and need an outlet for all of that heaviness;
- ❖ Because you feel safe behind your words on paper or the screen before you;
- ❖ Because you find clarity for yourself and your feelings through writing;
- ❖ Because you realize that maybe you're not the only one who has or is going through everything you've been through;
- ❖ Because perhaps with your words, you can spark change by inspiring strength, hope, and feeling in another;
- ❖ Because you need and want to heal;
- ❖ Because you realize you've already wasted too much time not trying;
- ❖ And lastly, because you realize how much you really do love writing and you have to start somewhere…

That was **ME!** I started to write, and it became my salvation and the beginning of my healing journey.

In a moment of transparency, I must admit I was terrified when I began to write because I do not have "fluffy tales of a perfect life." I write about the hardcore, scary shit nobody wants to hear and talk about—and I write about it honestly. After all, is there any other way to write the truth?

SO, SO, SO many times, I felt like throwing up as I read and reread my social media posts. *Could I really do it?* The questions kept coming to mind, with doubt and heaviness riding shotgun. Oh my…there's that heaviness again! ***"PUSH THE BUTTON! PUSH THE BUTTON AND DO IT!"*** I kept telling myself. And so starts the shaking…even **BEFORE** I push the button. ***"JUST PUSH THE BUTTON ALREADY!!!"***

CLICK

*"OH MY GOODNESS! Did I do the right thing? Oh no. Take it back! **TAKE IT BACK!!!**"*

Alas, I didn't.

One person reached. Two people reached. The number continues to climb. *"Oh my gosh! Did I really do the right thing? Well, it's out there now. There are no takebacks. I can't watch this. Log out,*

Laurie. Just log out and let it go however it is going to go."

At the time, all I could think about was how grateful I was not to have many people following my page. It was a mere 40 or so. My post couldn't reach too far with that small of a number, right? Thank goodness I had to go to work so that I could take my mind off of what I had done. Even more thankfully, come the end of that day, there were only a few likes and no haunting remarks. I logged on to find nothing but kindness. Wow! **KINDNESS!** *"Hmm… Okay. Maybe this isn't so bad!"*

I have to pause and think this thing through. Am I really willing to go all out and share my story? Once it's out there, it can open up a whole lot of… **NO! DON'T THINK ABOUT IT!** All of that negativity…it'd be so easy to stop now before…

NO! DON'T LET THE VOICE OF DOUBT WIN YOU OVER AND STOP YOU FROM TRYING!

Here comes that little voice again. *"What did I have to offer anyone, though? Why would anyone care about what I have to say? I mean, I'm really a nobody, right? Why would my writing matter? What could I possibly write about?"*

As it turns out, **PLENTY**.

Now, you might be thinking, *"Why would a person be so terrified to put themselves out there?"* Well, when you've lived a life such as mine, terror is all I've ever really known.

- ✓ Terror.
- ✓ Fear.
- ✓ Hurt.
- ✓ Substance abuse.
- ✓ Depression.
- ✓ Suicidal tendencies.
- ✓ Threats.
- ✓ Mistrust.
- ✓ Anger.
- ✓ Letdowns.
- ✓ Abuse.
- ✓ Anxiety.
- ✓ Unheard.
- ✓ Heaviness.

There it is **AGAIN!** Oh, that *HEAVINESS!*

From my very earliest memories, well into my adulthood, those feelings, thoughts, and actions haunted my days—nearly as much as the many breaths I have breathed. In the midst of it all, I have actually proven to myself time and again that if I really set my mind to doing something, I can achieve my goals.

Still, for every time I take one step forward, negativity is there trying to undo everything I've worked so hard for…to drag me back down to where I have spent my entire life.

Those dreaded moments of terror were alive and well. What if…? What will…? Can I really do this? The ever-haunting thoughts and voices of the past were now **YELLING** at me.

"**YOU ARE NOTHING!**"
"**YOU ARE A NOBODY!**"
"**NOBODY CARES WHAT YOU HAVE TO SAY!**"
"**YOU ARE A LIAR!**"
"**YOU ARE DAMAGED GOODS!**"
"**YOU DON'T HAVE THAT ALL-IMPORTANT PIECE OF PAPER [high school diploma]! GUESS WHAT? WITHOUT IT, YOU WON'T GET ANYWHERE!**"

It's time to silence that noise.

Why can't I have the good life? Not everyone in life has a 12th-grade education. Is it really that important? There are plenty of successful people who have never graduated. Why can I not be an exception? I am smart. I am capable. I have the desire to be a successful and accomplished writer and photographer.

Suddenly, there came that small whisper:

"Can I tell you something? Without trying, you can never succeed."

There it is! The tiniest glimmer of hope.

So, what is it that brought me to this moment in time? It actually started in my early 40s when I began researching The Law of Attraction and feeling as if I wasn't able to achieve its most important piece: Manifestation. I had so much work to do, both on and for myself, before "The Law" could begin to work for me. What I didn't realize was that as I began to write, I was starting to manifest everything I wanted and desired in my life.

Truthfully, this is where I have really begun to live. First, however, let me take you back to many, many years before I even found myself in **THIS** place…

Chapter 2

A Long, Long Time Ago

Shrouded by the secrecy of my own truths, lying deep within the darkest realms of my mind, what I do recall of my childhood days are not all memories I wish to have. They are the ones that lay hidden beneath the layers of lost memory that, as I slowly heal, make themselves known and reiterate my feelings of fear and terror when I realize they are not "just dreams"; rather, they are the thoughts that are unbeknownst to all, except for my inner child and the ones who inflicted pain on me.

It has been extremely challenging throughout my life to decipher the reality of my truths at times because even though I have never been officially diagnosed with any mental disorders, I know that I display some signs of Post-Traumatic Stress Disorder (PTSD). Dissociative Amnesia is another condition I can relate to, as days, months, and years are literally nonexistent in the recesses of my mind.

Distant memories flash through my mind like that of an old slide show, featuring captures of a very young child. With them are **NOT** the usual feelings of love and happiness. Instead, they bring on that overwhelming feeling of terror and heaviness.

Why would such a young child be so fearful? I only wish I could explain how I never felt truly loved for the vast majority of my life. Worse yet, it seems I have always carried with me that feeling of terror. The only love and happiness I experienced were between my sibling and I and even with that, I'm sure you can relate to my brief pause if you have siblings because let's face it: Most siblings love to hate each other. My sibling and I were no different.

It seemed the longer I was in this "incarnation," and as the years wore on, both the weight of the heaviness and the intensity of the terror grew with me as well. Like silent partners, "we" grew cautious of those closest to me from the very earliest age.

I think it is and was truthfully those most unsettling feelings that initially drove me to protect myself the best I could as I grew, yet there was another feeling attached to all of this…an uneasy and unearthly feeling…a feeling that I truly **DID NOT BELONG** here with "these" people—to include the woman from my past to whom I never felt an attachment. Who was she? I didn't feel that way about just her, though. Why, as such a young child, did I have no deep feelings of belonging or attachment to *ANYONE* in my life?

As the years progressed, a few new truths would eventually be divulged…sort of.

My very first images were of a woman yelling and waving a very large branch at me. Terrified, I jumped across the creek before me and ran away from her as fast as my young legs would carry me. There was also a robin's nest with its beautiful blue eggs. I was so worried, as I feared their mother would not find those poor unborn babies. The long, picturesque driveway was lined with towering, majestic Maple trees.

And yet another memory of me hiding—terrified and hiding—in the tall grass that was just beyond the driveway. Slowly, I crawled and made my way to the culvert intersecting at the end of the long driveway, not wanting to be found.

A series of more memories come and then dissipate through my thoughts over the years, but only a few. Why do I not remember more?

The enormous, beautiful beast named "Lady" was an ever-loving Saint Bernard. She brought joy and love to my heart until…he **SHOT** her. To my horror, he did so right in front of me. I vaguely recall a story of Lady being rabid. I will never know if that was the truth for the remainder of my life. I do hazily remember playing with her just the day before. On the day of that horrifying event, I begged for any other outcome, to no avail. There would be no different result.

Then, there was a boarded-up mine shaft we used to explore, my sibling taking extra care to be sure I was safe at all times. Some of the fondest images I had from that time of my life, coupled with the big, beautiful picture I had drawn just to please the woman of my past, but it seemed to only anger her profusely.

Another blank slate of time appears. Why do I have just bits and pieces here and there? Are those empty spaces the reason for the overwhelming terror and heaviness I carry?

Perhaps my answer will come one day.

Chapter 3

Another Sense of Time
(The Early School Years)

Cherished memories are few and far between, appearing only as highlights. Other images have haunted me for many years to follow, replaying in my mind like a bad movie that is too mature for a young child—yet there is still a great deal even through those years that remains completely null and void.

With eager anticipation, the day had finally arrived. It was my turn to go to school!

I wasn't certain what to expect, but I hoped it would give me some relief from the life I was growing through and the feelings I carried with me daily. Oh, how incredibly wrong I was!!! What I soon learned was how extremely cruel kids could truly be.

See, I was a stocky, red-haired, fair-skinned, freckle-faced girl whose hair was cut short like a boy. I was dressed like a boy and, when my temper got the best of me, could indeed fight like a boy, too!

But that was not *WHY* it all began…

Flashbacks of a child's **"worst first day of school EVER"** weren't just flashbacks for me. I actually had one of those days that set the tone for years to come. Unfortunately, I remember that day like it was yesterday.

Registering me for school took longer than expected, and the bell for class had already rung. It seemed like we spent an eternity sitting across the desk from the man in the office.

Suddenly, it came on like an unbearable weight; that heaviness. Oh, that **terror** and **heaviness**!

On my very first day of school, I entered the classroom late. I patiently waited through the embarrassing introduction, sat down, and then raised my hand to ask to use the restroom. The stoutly reply resonated through the room:

"No! You just arrived and were already late. You can and will wait until recess."

There was a major issue with that denial: **I COULDN'T WAIT FOR RECESS.** In fact, I raised my hand again and explained that I could not wait. Again, I was sharply told *"NO!"*

So, the inevitable happened. I had a most mortifying accident right then and there—in front of everyone—on my first day of school. Not only did I have to live through the torture of that incident for quite some time, but even worse yet, my meager lunch had been placed right below my desk, leaving me without lunch that day.

Now, one might think, *"Okay. You can move past that, right?"* Perhaps I could have, but as I said: Kids can be ruthless, especially when they are all trying to find their place in school and with the "in-crowd."

All morning long, kids ruthlessly picked on and tormented me for any reason they could then find. That became a day I would never forget…for many reasons.

Just before lunchtime came, the teacher eventually asked if anyone would spare any lunch for me. Only one spoke up. She was so pretty, so kind, and she smelled so clean—as if she had just been freshly-sprinkled in baby powder. Her big, beautiful blue eyes, tanned skin, and soft, dirty-blonde hair were absolutely stunning. I was a wee bit envious of her, but that feeling quickly faded when I saw her for the simply beautiful soul she was. Truthfully, her kindness, care, and love radiated even more than her physical beauty. She was a gentle soul and just the person I needed on that very day.

She and I shared her lunch, and she taught me how to play jacks. It was the very first time I had ever seen the game. Honestly, I was very grateful for her company. She was the very first person to extend **ANY** form of kindness to me up to that point, so I chose to repay her with the only thing I had to offer: my friendship.

Terrified, I asked her to be my best friend, for if she answered yes, my loyalty to her as a friend would be forever.

And there it came…my answer…

To my surprise, it was **YES!!!**

So, she and I built a friendship that has, indeed, lasted a lifetime. Yes, even now we are still friends, although we did lose contact for many years and don't talk as much as I would love to. Over the years, my feelings for her have never diminished. With my very deepest gratitude and thanks to her, I have never forgotten the power of kindness…**EVER.**

Over the years while attending school, we remained friends and became inseparable. We played together and learned from each other, yet there came a time when it became apparent to me that she and I did, in fact, lead very different lives.

I recall her family often spent time together doing various activities, where mine usually did very little together. Her family went to church often, and mine was very opposed to the methodology of the church. Even when I expressed interest in going with my friend, it was immediately not up for discussion.

We both had our own strengths and weaknesses in school and helped each other to learn the things we struggled with. Even with everything we shared and although we were best friends, I never told her all of the things going on behind closed doors. Why, you ask? Because I was more terrified of losing the only friend I ever had.

So, I carried my secrets alone and in silence.

As the years carried on, there were a few things I enjoyed while growing up, such as spelling. I loved writing and receiving letters. Oh! And handwriting, especially writing forms such as calligraphy. I wrote letters to family that lived far away, usually to the woman I knew as a grandmother. I always looked forward to her lengthy letters, waiting in eager anticipation of news from so far away and the responses to my inquisitive mind. Her letters were always scented and smelled wonderful.

I also had a passion for figure skating, so much so that I dreamt of becoming as good as the elegant Dorothy Hamill. I took lessons and became good enough to earn myself a single trophy. That accomplishment gave me a reason to be proud.

Even though I did have some good in my life, the feelings of heaviness and terror never subsided.

At one point during my young years, I became horribly terrified of water. I had been pushed into the local pool and did not know how to swim. It was a fear that would remain with me my entire life.

I also recall choosing the last childhood pet I would have. It was a kitten and, after some time, it had to be put down because it had been "poisoned." Now, maybe it is just my thought, but why was it that each time a pet became a part of my life, it would die from "unfortunate causes"? That is something I have never stopped wondering about my entire life.

In fact, there are a few things I have never ceased to wonder about over the course of time…

Like why I never remember seeing a doctor, even when I was deathly ill with both Red and German measles. As I reflect, that was the only time in my entire childhood that I truly ever felt cared for by the woman. She sat by my bedside with a cold cloth and brought me ginger ale and toast for what seemed like days.

It probably was.

As a matter of fact, I don't ever recall seeing a dentist either. What I do know was that by the time I did see one, I needed **27 fillings!**

It has been my experience in life that sometimes, we never get the answers to our questions.

Laurie Benoit

Chapter 4

Woman or Child?

For a very short time, a small sense of relief formed in my heart, granting me some peace. It was when I recall the woman being gone for some time (it seemed to me that she was actually gone for quite a bit...weeks, perhaps). That wasn't the first time; neither was it the last.

Why did it take her **absence** for me to feel at ease?

There have not been many moments in my life when I can recall a moment of peace, so when those moments appeared, they stood out ever so significantly.

What I remember being told about the circumstances of her absence was that it was my fault she had left. Honestly, I was glad she was gone—no matter the reason. I actually swore I would be a better kid if she *DIDN'T* come back.

See, I often did not express my thoughts or feelings because I never felt safe enough to. On that day, however, I broke down, opened up my heart, and said exactly what I felt.

That was the same day I was told that the woman **WAS NOT** my mother. Without a doubt, I *BELIEVED* it!

As the conversation continued, the things I was told only opened my mind to many more thoughts and questions:

Where was my mother?

Did she not love me?

Why and how could she just leave me here?

When did she leave?

I don't remember her!!!

Strangely enough and truth be told, in the deepest pits of my stomach, I had always felt that the woman was not my mother. There was always an awful lack of connection with her, leaving me to question why it was that way.

Finally, I at least had something I could understand.

On that day, many things in my life changed, with the truth of my mother only tipping the scales of my thoughts. That was one of the most traumatic days of my life. It was also the day I remember that the innocence of a child was taken.

What I endured that day still haunts my thoughts, dreams, and emotions as if it all happened yesterday. After it was over, I was told one thing: I should never do with anyone else what I had done on that day.

Truth be told, to this very day, I have never been able to do any of those things with another because it has literally replayed over and over again in my mind…with a disgusting repulsiveness.

After that day, my memories were no longer "just memories." They became actual living nightmares. I started to understand why I felt such a disconnection, sickness, loneliness, shattered, isolated, and neglected.

Enter in that unbearable heaviness again!

With what I endured on that day, it literally opened up the gates of Hell within my mind. Memories flashed through my mind of all the other incidents of similarity. I puked. I awoke in the middle of the night, crying about the horrors of my reality, and I puked some more.

To my dismay, soon after that woman came back, everything resumed as it had before — only I felt not only hurt, but also angry, disappointed, and carried an even more oppressive terror. I then began to feel that everything and everyone in my life was conditional…and a lie. I felt used, dirty, impure, and repulsed by what happened to me.

What I learned from the experience was that trust did not exist, as my deepest thoughts and feelings had been shared. Thoughts of leaving entered my mind. I no longer believed I would be safe from the repercussions of sharing what I had. I was terrified at the thought of leaving, but what would be worse? *To stay?*

I recall acting out after the incident because I no longer felt safe. Worse yet, I didn't know who I could tun to. I started pushing back and truthfully, I didn't care how much. The pain was etched deep in my soul. I just wanted the feelings to **GO AWAY.** I wanted to be *LOVED*.

Now, as a parent, I know all children like to push the boundaries to determine what one's limits are or how much one can get away with. What would **YOU** consider excessive for spanking a child? I will tell you this one thing: As a parent myself, I believed a swat on the butt was spanking enough. I'm sure you'll understand why soon enough.

The belt. In my days of growing up, when you got the belt, you were in some serious trouble.

For me, as I recall, the spankings were so frequent, I grew numb to the pains *AND* the lessons. However, I suppose looking back, I shouldn't have been so bold to say so because then, I felt like the woman took it as a challenge to find something new that **DID** cause me pain and **DID** teach me a lesson.

She kept trying different weaponry, only to have each continuously break under her connection with my bare skin. Eventually, she did find something that hurt: a well-used boot jack. After a few uses of her hitting me hard enough to leave welts, I recall even ***THAT*** broke.

So, she bought a new one.

I vaguely remember that soon after, the spankings became a regular occurrence.

I started smoking, and it was inevitable that I would get caught. I was still very young and had only one source to supply my newfound habit: the woman's stash. I felt I needed something to help alleviate my stress!

As soon as it was found out that I was smoking, I was forced to sit down and smoke a carton of cigarettes, a package of Colts, and a couple of White Owl cigars. I smugly took it as a challenge to finish them—and did just that. In response, smoking became an almost lifelong habit of helping to alleviate the continuing stressors in my life.

As the flashbacks of some of my repressed memories came to bear in my foremost thoughts, replaying over and over again like a broken record along with the genuine loathing I had for the woman, I started to prepare to get myself out of the situation.

Chapter 5

Hope for a New Life

At some time in our lives, we all like to think the grass is greener on the other side of the fence. Do we not?

Well, I was no different (at least that truly was my hope). I had grown old for my young age. You're probably thinking *"GROWN OLD???"* Yes. **OLD**. At a very young age, I was already tired and living a life of terror. The heaviness that enveloped me for most of my days was unbearably overwhelming. I knew something had to change because frankly, I just couldn't take it anymore.

So, I turned to the law in hopes it would protect me as a child.

What. In. The. HELL. Was. I. Thinking???

I explained the circumstances of my visit to the Law Enforcement that day and showed them the punishment I received for eating a piece of pie from the two freshly-made pies that were sitting out. I was covered with bruises and had two black eyes and a broken nose — *and nothing would be done?!!*

They just took me back there…to endure more.

So, I did what I thought was best: I ran. I packed clothes, food, took money, and **RAN**. I was smart and did not stay in one place for more than two nights in a row. I kept my clothes at school in my locker. Yes, I did say 'school.' They hadn't bothered to look for me there. I think they thought I wasn't bold enough to show my face at school. Truthfully, I only went there for warmth, to wash up in the restrooms, and to change clothes. It was there that they caught me…the first time.

Needless to say, I had learned my lesson about that. I clearly remember the consequences of my actions, and they were *GREAT*. Not only was I punished at school with the strap; I also endured more punishment afterward.

I'm uncertain how long it was after that before I planned my next escape, but I was even more certain to be better prepared. Before I left, I was sure to eye a few possible locations where I could stay, so I knew where to take my things.

That time, I brought food, cigarettes, a credit card, blanket, pillow, and warmer clothes.

I am unsure how long I was gone, but I recall it getting cold much earlier. Finding warm places to sleep became a challenge. One night, with a stroke of luck, I found an unlocked trailer. How long I stayed in that one place, I cannot remember. I do know I began to get comfortable and, of course, what happens when one gets too comfy?

One could easily say I got careless. I had overslept, and someone caught me leaving the trailer one morning. She was a child not much older than I. *Could I talk to and befriend her? And, if I did manage to do so, would I be able to trust her?* She quickly pushed me back into the trailer and, when I realized why, I couldn't do anything but thank her afterward.

Her mom was on her way out to work. So that I would not be caught, she shoved me back into the trailer and quickly blurted out an excuse to her mom about her presence there. She then waited until her mother left to join me in the trailer. She asked me to tell her how I came to be there, in their trailer?

I told her the truth…mostly. I did not tell her my real name for fear she would call the place I left in terror. I did, however, share with her the rest of my truths. She empathized with me and told me she would give me a couple of days to move on because her mother would not be understanding and would definitely want me **GONE**.

So, as much as I did not want to have to look for another place, I began my search again. I searched for other homes that had trailers first and found only one. I really did not want to stay there, though, because it was only a few houses away from the place I wanted to be **VERY** far away from. It was sheltered in a carport, so I slept inside for only a few nights. Then, one night upon my return, I found it had been locked! The same carport also housed lounge chairs (the kind one would put out in the Summer to lay on), so I chose to sleep on one of them after finding out I could not get back into the trailer. I was so tired and hungry, I did not want to hunt for yet another place to sleep that late at night. I curled up on the lounger and slept.

I slept so soundly, I awoke late to the sound of someone stirring in the house. I was too late! I saw one person and then a second peer through the lit window above me. Suddenly, the door that was only a few feet away from me flew open!

I was terrified! I looked the man over and thought to myself, *"I can't do this anymore. I can't keep running."* I was so tired, so in need of a shower, and **SO** famished. I again told my story of mostly the truth, as they fed me some toast and waited for Child Protective Services (CPS) to show up and talk to me.

When CPS interviewed me, I told them the **WHOLE** truth so that they could remove my sibling as well. They didn't do that, though! Even with my pleas for their help, they refused. To my utter despair, they left my sibling in the home.

I was then taken to an office in a neighboring town where I was interviewed over and over again, taken to a hospital to be examined, and then finally taken to what I later came to know as a "Receiving Home." Meanwhile, I continued to beg and plead for them to go back and remove my sibling, for I deeply feared for their safety and knew they would be punished in my absence. CPS never heeded my words.

Oh, my word! There it is **AGAIN!** That unbearable heaviness—only now it was accompanied by **guilt**, **anger**, **sadness**, and **fear** for the truths I had just divulged. A deep feeling of utter sickness of what would become of my sibling—the only person I truly felt any attachment to—sent my life into a whirlwind of broken emotions.

Chapter 6

A New Beginning?

Doubt. Doubt had become a dominating thought as it raced through my heart and mind like a runaway train bound for nowhere.

Trust was second in line, eating away at me like an out-of-control storm of darkness, stripping away at my very soul. Trust in myself as well as others plagued my emotions.

Did I do the right thing? How could I get them to take my sibling now? I wouldn't be there to prove what was going on behind those closed doors. The definitely won't send me back now. ***WHY DID THEY NOT COME WITH ME???*** We could have been safe together.

Like an earthquake, the next few years contained consistent instability and left me feeling as if I was walking on shaky ground.

My life of revolving doors and the endless unpacking had only just begun. All I had was a small suitcase (not even filled with clothing), and a mind, heart, and soul filled to their peak with horrors. That was what my life consisted of, along with nobody whatsoever in which to confide.

Oh, how I missed my dear friend! Would even she understand all of the heaviness I carried with me? If only I had told her what I was going through, what I would do, and why. Truthfully, this would only be the beginning of me missing her throughout the entirety of my years to follow.

Regret had also become another silent partner along the way. I did not regret leaving, though. I regretted not being able to convince my sibling of their imminent danger. Why did they not listen to me? Because I was the younger one? Perhaps I will never understand.

And so began the journey to find my family and the place I thought I was meant to be. Home, after home, after home, after home. Was there not a home and family just for me? Someone who could love me unconditionally, even though I was so damaged and imperfect? Someone who could forgive me, even when I was learning and making mistakes? I mean, one doesn't go from being completely messed up to knowing how just to be normal, do they? Maybe it's just me. Maybe I **WAS** just an awful kid who didn't deserve love.

It seemed that no matter what home I was in, if I felt safe and loved, I self-destructed it by harming another or I was tormented at school to the point of me losing that fiery temper of mine.

There were many endless days of torture from school kids and foster siblings alike in most places. The truth about how absolutely downright cruel kids are couldn't be any more real in my life. I thought the kids back home had been ruthless. Oh, how very wrong I was. I experienced a whole new level of torture. There were many days I was told that nobody loved me or wanted me because I was damaged, ugly, and obviously a despicable child who, apparently, even my own family couldn't stand. Those mean and hurtful comments were incessant.

Now, I knew some of those words weren't true. Those words didn't really hurt me, but the ones that ***DID*** surely did their damage. Add on the pushing, poking, cutting of my hair, tripping, and so on, and my anger was fueled all the more.

I just longed to be loved and accepted. **THAT WAS ALL!**

I recall at one point, I had a really wonderful social worker who became a part of my endless cycle of doorways. She gifted me a journal and talked with me about all the things that were happening. She listened as I told her everything in truth and tried to determine why I was having such problems in all of the placements I had been.

I appreciated her, for she was kind, caring, and really listened to me. I used the journal to unload some of my heaviness along the way. I suppose she expected I would do just that. Finally, I had a place to share what I felt when I couldn't talk to her. With my silent friend, I shared my deepest, darkest thoughts and feelings about each passing doorway I would enter and exit.

Wouldn't you know it? Like everything else in my life, my journal became something I was scrutinized about. Every single word within, I had to justify. Everything I felt and shared in the book was read and used against me in the worst possible ways, leaving me feeling vulnerable, unsafe, and uncertain of what would become of me.

I'm not sure how long after I was in the endless circle of revolving doors before I was sent (the first time) to spend some time in a hospital. Truthfully, I'm not even certain how long I remained there. What I do know of it now is that I had been admitted for "play therapy" — probably to determine what my life entailed up to that point in time.

Inevitably, I was returned to the cycle of never-ending revolving doors and endless unpacking.

That was until one day, I was returned to the only foster home where I ever felt love. Well, let me tell you from experience that a child who has never truly felt loved does **NOT** know what to do and how to act when they *DO* begin to feel loved. As for me, I did the unspeakable.

I hurt another, showing love and care in the only way I knew how. The disgusting truths of what love looked like in my life became quite evident in all of its sickness.

And so, the judgments began again. I was both shown and told that I was damaged and could not and would not be accepted with my flaws. I wasn't even given a chance to say how very sorry I was—to say how disgusted and disappointed I was with myself for my own behavior. I was never given an opportunity to prove how sorry I had felt.

For many years, I have carried with me the sadness, heaviness, and guilt of hurting someone I hadn't realized I was hurting so long ago, all because I truly did not know how to handle goodness and love in my young life.

The consequence of my action was that I was removed from that place and not allowed to return…**EVER**.

I was then placed in an emergency placement. After only a short time, I was asked if I thought I could behave in a home with my sibling?

WHAT DID THEY MEAN???

To my utter shock and surprise, they had finally removed my sibling from the place where we had grown up—the place I begged and pleaded for them to take him from when I had left!

WHY WAS IT THAT I WAS JUST HEARING ABOUT THIS NOW???

Chapter 7

To Be or Not to Be

Like an out-of-control cyclone, thoughts and questions **MORE THAN** inundated my mind. There was no way to stop the infinite possibilities of what happened from roaring through the recesses of my brain. There was so much between us that I believed needed to be said and understood.

OF COURSE, I wanted to be and live with the only person who could truly understand the full depths of our lives behind those closed doors. *YES! YES! YES!* Perhaps we could grow and be loved as we deserved to be…

Sadly, I had misconceived entirely how my own sibling might have felt about seeing me. I hadn't even considered what they might have thought when they were told I would be coming to live with them. I was just so excited about having them back in my life and hoped we could rekindle our childhood affection while growing through the rest of our lives together.

What I also hadn't considered was that our relationship would never ever be the same.

I did end up moving there, but like every other doorway I entered, I soon found myself leaving again. I don't recall the length of time I spent there. I do, however, know that I was moved when I began having problems at school again.

I guess it just wasn't meant to be.

Just when I thought the endless stream of opened and closed doors was beginning all over again, what I didn't know was that there was only one place left willing to take me in. This awful child who was unworthy of love and a family had one more chance to find her family and forever home.

The visit with the new family was a bit longer, as the worker did her best to confirm that some of my requests would be met before she left me there. She was assured that they would honor those requests.

No sooner than the door shut behind me, I wanted out of there. I wanted to **RUN**. I had a sick gut feeling that I was going to heavily regret being there. There was a language barrier that made me uncomfortable (to say it lightly). Within only a couple of hours, my gut instincts were proven correct.

My new siblings were expected to show me where we were to catch the bus the next day. They did as they were told. However, along with that, they also told me how things were and what was expected of me. I was to keep to myself, keep my head down, and not talk to anyone…or else suffer the consequences. I was shoved around, told how rotten and ugly I was, and then told that if I said anything, I would pay for it in ways I would never forget.

For whatever the reason, I believed them.

Upon our return to the house, my new siblings claimed I had made threats against two of them and that they feared being near me. I was then shown my new makeshift room, where I spent the remainder of that day. The room was made up of three solid walls and one that I could move that was next to another room. A piece of drywall was put in place the give the impression of a fully-built room. It was also the source of the reason why I experienced more terror and made me want out of there all the more.

From my very first day on the bus, my siblings made certain nobody would talk to me. They spread awful rumors that their home was the last resort for me because I was nothing but an unwanted, terrible child whose natural family couldn't stand. No, it wasn't the truth, but it cut through my heart like someone had just shredded it into a million pieces.

As a child in the foster care system, feelings of isolation are easily built upon misunderstanding, miscommunication, bullying, and **ALL** of the experiences within the system itself.

As the days went by and time passed, I loathed that place more than the place I came from before my foster journey started. I was never racist towards anyone, but I truly despised that family. They had the audacity to speak of me at dinner every night…in their native language! That went on until I was able to understand them. The longer I was there, the more I grew to hate them—and the more they refused me contact with my worker.

One evening at dinner, there was a knock at the door. It was the police. When my siblings and I inquired about why they had arrived, we were told they were bringing someone new to the home. Later that night, the person arrived. They were much older than the rest of us and, truth be told, I didn't understand why they came to stay there.

I had an extremely uneasy feeling when I found out that they, too, would be staying in the basement with me in the room with the adjoining door. It was the beginning of a new terror in a place I already hated. Each day and night provided an endless supply of horror. I needed out of there, and **I NEEDED OUT IMMEDIATELY!!!**

The heaviness and terror, along with all of my other silent partners, became excruciatingly challenging to carry anymore, so I asked the school to call my social worker. I expressed that I did not feel safe in the home and needed to move. After talking with the worker on the phone, she came to the home—much to the surprise of the adults—and removed me. From that day forth, I was never placed in another foster home.

Chapter 8

Just a Small-Town Girl

Uncertainty, excitement, uneasiness, fear, and heaviness were what I felt as the social worker and I traveled the highway. The drive to the city wasn't that long, but I had never lived in nor seen that much of a city before. It was kind of thrilling for me because I had always been just a small-town girl.

City life would definitely prove to be a whole new chapter. It wasn't just the city itself; it was also **WHERE** I was going to live.

The new place had a priest, nuns, more adults, a doctor, and a whole **LOT** of kids…30 or maybe even more. There were four houses with kids and adults in each. I attended a regular school and was expected to walk there and back every day. *"It's better than taking the bus every day,"* I thought to myself.

I seem to recall not having as many problems fitting in there. All of the kids were more like me. They didn't fit into the stream of endless doorways either. By this time, I had already entered and exited 33 doors without finding a place to call "home." The new place is what I considered home until I began to feel safe again…and then I inevitably self-destructed. Why, you might be thinking? Well, that truth will come shortly.

The heaviness rose to the top again…that unbearable heaviness.

As best as I can recall, I had been there for over a year and met some really wonderful people—adults and kids alike. In fact, I had even made a couple of really good friends while at school, too, but they weren't as dear to me as my friend from home. Out of the years in the stream of endless doorways, it was there that I stayed the longest.

On more than one occasion while I lived in that place, there were invitations and talk of a few different families going through the strides to adopt me after having regular visits with me. I sincerely hoped that something would have come out of it all but to no avail.

I was later told they fell through because my birth family refused to sign the papers. I had been gone for so long from them. Why would they not sign? Better yet, why would or should they had even had any say? Instead, I became a permanent ward of the court.

WHY? Why was I not allowed to be with a family who was willing to have me and *NOT* treat me like I had been in the other foster homes? I suppose the answer was simple: I guess I didn't deserve to be loved. I didn't deserve to be part of a family who wouldn't do those things to me…to US. I guess maybe I was just an awful, ugly, unworthy, unwanted child after all.

I COULDN'T TAKE IT ANYMORE! WHY??? So many questions, thoughts, and feelings took over like a tornado spinning out of control while eating its way through a barren land.

Not long after that revelation, I ran away from that facility. With the help of another girl, we both packed up and left. The next few days are a blur. All I can remember is that incessant, unbearable weight I carried, the fear of getting caught, and all of the feelings that had built up for so many years. Tack on the shame of not even being allowed to have a family to call my own and who would treat me right, and I was a bundle of nerves.

The one thing I do recall is the two bottles of pills I took from the bathroom cabinet to ingest. I was **DONE**. I didn't want to **LIVE** anymore. I didn't want to **ENDURE** any more *PAIN*. I felt incredibly old, tired, and just **DONE**! I no longer wanted to remember those awful horrors. I didn't want to keep carrying the heaviness. I refused to keep trying. Why should I? I had nothing left to offer or give. What was the point of me trying? All of my efforts had been for nothing, it seemed. Even my own sibling wanted nothing more to do with me. I took the pills, in hopes of never waking up again.

Only I did… I awakened in a hospital. I have no recollection of where I was when I took the pills nor the trip to the hospital. I do remember waking up in the hospital with an extremely sore throat and stomach. I vaguely recall seeing a doctor in the Emergency Room. I was then sent to the Psychiatric Ward to determine whether or not my suicide attempt was real.

OH, YES! IT WAS REAL!

I spent four months in the hospital on a waitlist before being transferred to a Children's Psychiatric Ward elsewhere in the city. It was a locked facility—one I would remain in for about a year.

During that time, my birth mother made her first of many appearances in my life. Much like the many endless doorways I encountered, that was how our relationship was; an endless stream of brief appearances. Just what I needed: another form of instability in my life. That was also the year my education stopped for most of the remainder of my life, leaving me with an incomplete junior high school education.

I dealt with some serious issues while in that locked facility because throughout the years, I had talked about my growing through the system and, when I finally tried to end my life, **THEN** they wanted to know what made me "tick"?! I was *DONE* with talking and trying to be heard. It hadn't done me any good after all of those years, so what would talking change about my situation? Oh! And we were expected only to talk and not lose our shit because the moment we did lose it, we were "rewarded" with isolation and a needle filled with Largactil—a medication used to treat behavioral problems. If one needle didn't do the trick, we would have another dose.

What really angered me was that after all the years in care, they dared to wonder what was wrong! They **DIDN'T** damn well listen and, in my opinion, they obviously didn't care to listen until I couldn't damn well take anymore.

I spent so long there *NOT* sharing that truthfully, I could tell you word-for-word everything the psychiatrist would ask and say. Even now, I could manipulate a psychiatrist or psychologist into believing that anything I shared with them would be enough to have them send me away, thinking I have my shit together and don't need them.

There is, however, one major downfall to that: I couldn't get the help I so desperately needed. Honestly, I didn't' until many years later—in my own time.

Anyway, I was done talking. Anything I had to say had already been said and dismissed just as quickly. So, what did I do? You guessed correctly if you said, *"SHE RAN!"*

With sirens blaring, police dogs barking, and lights flashing, **I RAN**. To avoid my scent being picked up by the dogs, I ran towards the sprinklers I heard clack-clack-clacking off in the distance. Barefoot, cold, and wet, I made my way to the place I thought best to hide: the cold, callous streets of the city's downtown core. It was a place that would become "home" for me for years to follow.

Chapter 9

Once in a Lifetime

In the dark of the night, I ran as my bare feet pounded against the cold pavement. I stopped only when I absolutely had to. I kept going as quickly as I could to get as far away from the facility as possible.

I can't say what time it was when I finally reached my destination, but I do know I was **SO** tired. I searched vehemently for a spot to sleep. Although it was Summer, I was cold and damp from my journey. I found a covered doorway and drifted off to sleep.

At the break of light and for days after, I wandered the streets aimlessly searching for other runaways and street people. Occasionally, I would panhandle for a bit of change to buy something to eat. Eventually, I had a stroke of luck and ran into some kind people. One, in particular, invited me to her home to shower, gave me some clothes, and offered me a modest meal—all of which I gratefully accepted.

As time went by, I found out information as to where all the different groups of street people hung out. I befriended people from those different groups so as to not necessarily be around the same people all the time. Sometimes, I hung out with male prostitutes; other times, I was able to score some drugs to sell. At one point, I started working the streets, pulling a few tricks here and there to make ends meet.

I learned to numb some of my pain with alcohol and drugs and was able to finally support my smoking habit. What I also found out was that I could afford a roof over my head from pulling tricks…most of the time. I, along with one other **VERY** young girl *(she was only **ten** years old)*, refused to work for any of the pimps that dealt with and handled the young girls. The pimps often beat and drugged them, kept their money, and isolated them from all the other street people. Worse yet, many were shipped to other cities, never to return. I was **NOT** having that happen to her or me!

Everything was going quite well for the young girl and me until the day an angry pimp threatened both of our lives. The girl immediately left and returned home. I, on the other hand, had nowhere else to go. So, firstly, I tried to rally support with some of the street people I had come to know. Not much luck there, as most did not want to contend with the pimp. While I made my rounds, he had already started hunting me. When he did catch up to me, he pulled a gun on me. It was then I decided it was time for me to equal the playing field.

So, in talking to one friend, he explained he had a contact he could put me in touch with to procure a weapon of my own. My mind was deadset: I would end that pimp's life if need be. In my opinion, the time in jail would have been worth getting him off the street, for I knew some of the terrified girls he had under his control who were afraid for their very lives. They had shared with me their awful horrors, so I not only carried my own heaviness but theirs as well.

My friend made the introduction as agreed. That night, we met at my friend's home. I don't recall how I got there **(*damn this Dissociative Amnesia!*)**, but when I arrived, the room was unlit. My friend invited me in, did the introduction, and quickly left us alone to talk.

The man was tall and lanky with dark hair and brooding eyes that peered at me. I was certain he could see right through me. We sat in darkness all night as I explained to him my story and how the pimp held others I knew in a form of captivity. I talked so long that eventually, I fell asleep safe and sound in his arms. He held me there all night. When I awoke, he told me he would not give me an answer until the next day, only **AFTER** he had time for careful consideration of my request.

What I wasn't at all prepared for was his final answer: **NO.** No, he would not procure a firearm for me.

There it was again…that **heaviness** and terror—of *EPIC* proportions!

What came from his mouth next were words that I felt I had no choice but to accept:

"Instead of getting you a firearm, I will offer you a place to lay low until we can get you out of this mess."

And so, with slight hesitation, I accepted that once-in-a-lifetime opportunity, as well as the lifelong friendship he also extended to me over the years, even to today. He has always been too humble to ever admit he saved my life, but he did.

I could have ended up dead or living a life in jail. Instead, he offered me a new life—one that granted me freedom.

Soon after my "relocation," word of the pimp's demise hit the street. No, I'm not the one to blame. Call it karma or whatever you'd like, but he was in a fatal car crash not long after pulling a gun on me. Word spread quickly, but not fast enough to free the girls he had under his control. Sadly, another pimp had picked up all of them.

I stayed with my friend for some time, though at times, I know I was extremely difficult to deal with. Although I was technically a teen, deep down inside, I was still that angry child from the life I had grown through. So, just like those other times when I felt safe, cared for, and even loved, I tried to self-destruct my circumstance. **UNLIKE** the other times, he surprised me by accepting me—flaws and all.

I started writing bits and pieces of my thoughts and feelings while I lived with him. He, in turn, expressed his honest opinions about those writings. He always told me I should write, but I sloughed it off because I truly didn't believe my words were anything extraordinary.

What I wouldn't know until many years later was that he saved some of my writings until I was ready for and could appreciate them.

I don't recall how or even when we parted ways but eventually, we did. From there, my life continued to dive into more downward spirals and a host of negativity.

Chapter 10

Life Isn't Fair

At some point in our lives, we decide we're going to be an adult and grow up, right? Some may choose to settle down, enter a relationship, and live life. However, when a person has lived with and through abuse their entire life, it often doesn't change, and the cycle continues until a person decides that they are going to change their outlook on life. Sadly, many don't.

While still a teen and after parting ways with my dear friend, I chose to give a relationship a try. That ended swiftly and abruptly when I caught my boyfriend cheating.

My next relationship led me to severe alcoholism while I endured years of physical abuse. Black eyes, bruises, continuously being kicked out of places, and hospital visits were my "norm." I finally left him, but not long after, he found out where I had moved to. He showed up drunk, broke in, and almost killed me. That day, he dove at me with a butcher knife in his hand and tried to stab me while I laid on my bed reading a book. As he came at me, I put both of my feet in the air and kicked him, slamming him into the wall and breaking his ribs. Terrified, I left and didn't return for months. When I did, it was only to retrieve my belongings.

The downward spiral of relationships continued for many years to come, looking for what, I wasn't certain. Each contained different forms of abuse:

- ✓ Financial.
- ✓ Physical.
- ✓ Emotional.
- ✓ Verbal.
- ✓ Psychological.
- ✓ I even witnessed Child Abuse towards my own children.

For me, the verbal abuse did the worst damage to me in life. All of the flashbacks and memories of every nasty, rotten word weighed me down like I was drowning in quicksand.

Hell, being honest here: I was no angel in any of my relationships because I had no clue how to heal, communicate, cope, or move past everything life had dealt me. Strangely enough, I knew what I **DIDN'T** want in my life, and that was everything I had endured not only as a child but also as I grew into a woman.

I was messed up. I still carried with me those silent partners I had grown "attached" to and that unbearable heaviness remained. Oh, that heaviness!

All the while, there was still the random appearances from my mother throughout the years, with years of neglect in between—at least that's how I felt. Even now as I write these very words, her presence in my life is void because I believe I just don't measure up to her standards. **HER** love has always been conditional. I love my mother, but truthfully, it seems I'm better off not having her in my life because I just never know when she'll leave again or why. What would I do so wrong the next time?

At one point, when I had been fighting to get my kids back from the very system that failed me, a wise woman was injected into my life. Although she shared a great deal of advice and many words, there was a series of words that were etched into my thoughts. No truer words applied to anyone else than me:

LIFE ISN'T FAIR.

With those three words, my focus changed. I knew what she said was true: *LIFE ISN'T FAIR.* The more I thought about it, the more I realized those words were not just about me; they were about everyone. Everyone has shit to deal with; it's just different for each of us. It was then I truly realized life wasn't just about "poor Laurie"; it was about the kids that would one day (hopefully) look up to me. After all, one day, they, too, would have their own shit to deal with.

As the years passed, I matured. When I wasn't prepared or even looking for a love interest, I met someone. He accepted **ME** — the imperfect **ME**, the vulnerable **ME**, the scared **ME**, the **ME** who carried so many years of pain, the whole **ME** with all of my flaws. He, too, was flawed and imperfect just like **ME**, but he stayed with **ME**. In fact, he is my husband and has been for 15 years to date. Without him, I couldn't begin to tell you where I'd be right now. I am glad he is here because there is no place I'd rather be than home.

Something else made a dramatic shift in my life, too. When I began to feel safe and loved, instead of self-destructing, I began to write. Initially, I penned poetry for a short while. Then, I believed I was ready to share my life story…but honestly, I wasn't.

I would begin writing and have to stop when the signs of PTSD started to show again. There were moments when I violently thrashed in the middle of the night and cried in my sleep behind the reoccurring flashbacks. Some of those hidden horrors surfaced and sent me into terror before realizing I wasn't just having a nightmare. Those things really happened to *ME*.

I stopped writing for a number of years until the flashbacks subsided and the nightmares ceased. When I eventually felt safe to do so, I started again and took baby steps. I also looked into The Law of Attraction. I researched it and tried to implement it into my life, only to find myself feeling disappointed because everything I read led me to believe I could **NOT** manifest what I wanted in my life. Why? Because I had so much to *heal* from.

As a direct result, I began writing, meditating, and looking after **ME** when I needed to. In addition, I started my Laurie Benoit Facebook Fan Page and began to write about my experiences to bring awareness, share insight, and bring hope and comfort to others who may be coping with even just *ONE* thing I have endured. I have a purpose: To inspire others to share their story and to begin the healing process. Instead of trying to tackle a whole book, I chose to talk about one subject or group of events at a time. Slowly, I noticed that the people who were meant to come into my life did just that. The situations that were meant to open did just that. In the process, I began to **HEAL**. At this very moment, I am still healing.

It has been a journey that has brought me so much more than I could have ever hoped for, for it was only through my healing journey that I can truly understand…

THE TRANSFORMATIVE POWER OF THE WORD.

About the Author

Laurie Benoit is a wife and mother of four, residing in the small village of Climax, Saskatchewan (Canada) where she rekindled her lifelong love of writing and photography. Since 2014, she has become an International Best-Selling Author as a contributor to *God Says I am Battle-Scar Free: Testimonies of Abuse Survivors – Part Four*, a Blogger, and a Freelance Writer. In her new book, *The Transformative Power of "The Word,"* she takes you on a journey through life's hardships and self-discovery with the purpose to inspire others to lead a more fulfilling life, despite one's obstacles.

Appendix

Maharaj, N. (n.d.) Retrieved April 2, 2019 from: http://www.nisargadatta.net/

Laurie Benoit

Made in the USA
Monee, IL
20 July 2020